Growing Blueberries

by Vladimir G. Shutak and Robert E. Gough

CONTENTS

Introduction

Between the two of us we have about 40 years experience in growing highbush blueberries in Rhode Island. We have read and published a lot of scientific papers about this plant. We have also killed a few dozen plants trying to improve their growth and production, but we believe that we have learned a few things in the process and would like to share them with you.

Would you like to grow blueberries in your own yard and enjoy fresh fruit for 8 to 10 weeks during the summer? You can, if you collect a few basic guidelines about location, soil, and culture. We will tell you how to do it all in this bulletin.

You know that there are a lot of different kinds of blueberries besides the highbush blueberry — dryland, evergreen, mountain, rabbiteye, half-high, and low bush. We are going to talk about the highbush blueberry only — the kind most common to commercial growers and the home gardener.

Highbush blueberry plants are easy to grow, relatively pestfree, and need little maintenance; they also fit very easily into most landscape plans. The plant has delicate white bell-shaped flowers in the spring, delicious fruit in the summer, bright crimson leaves in the fall, and red or yellow-colored branches in the winter.

Where Can You Grow Blueberries?

Highbush blueberries can be grown in most areas of the United States; however, don't plant them in an area where winter temperatures frequently fall below –20°F. Also, because they need winter chilling, don't plant blueberries in areas where there is not at least 800 hours (about 2 months) of temperatures below 40°F. You can extend these limits somewhat by planting new cultivars especially developed for extreme northern and southern areas. In most cases these cultivars are crosses between highbush blueberry and rabbiteye for southern locations and low bush blueberry for northern locations.

Beating the Climate Limitations

You can extend the general temperature area limitations if you select a location within your area which is known to be warmer or cooler than the surrounding area — this is called a microclimate.

For instance, if you have an area protected from the cold northern winds, it will be warmer than an exposed area. It will also reduce drying injury. You can create an area like this by providing a windbreak by planting trees or putting up a fence on the north side of the planting. Frequently, you can also take advantage of existing windbreaks provided by buildings — yours or your neighbors.

Any structure — even a driveway — near your plants which absorbs and/or reflects heat, may help to maintain higher temperatures. If you are looking for a cooler area, select an exposed area with good air movement. A northern slope or an area which is shaded from the late afternoon sun (after 3:00 P.M.) will provide a cooler environment.

Reduce Frost Damage

If you live in an area where late spring frosts are likely, locate the plants on a northern slope. This will delay the bloom in the spring and reduce chances of frost damage. A gentle slope is also recommended because it will provide better air drainage, help dry the air, and reduce fungus diseases. Do not plant in areas surrounded by buildings or dense stands of trees because both will cause poor air circulation.

Provide Full Sunlight

For best production, plant your plants where they can receive 8 hours of sunlight per day. Too much shade results in spindly growth, reduces yield, and decreases the quality of the fruit.

Green Manure Crops

A green manure crop is usually a small grain crop that is tilled under before it matures. The decaying tops and roots provide organic matter and some nutrients to help build up the soil. This process increases soil aeration, water-holding capacity, and stimulates microbial activity in the soil.

Some of these grains grow best in summer and will not tolerate a frost. Others will survive the winter and are useful in preventing soil erosion during this time. Some commonly used green manure crops are listed below, along with their time and rate of seeding.

Crop	Seeding Time	Seeding Rate per 1,000 sq. ft.	Time to Turn Under
Winter rye	Early fall	2 lb.	Very early spring
Buckwheat	Early summer	1 lb.	Early fall
Ryegrass	Early fall	½ lb.	Early spring
Millet	Early summer	1 lb.	Early fall
Soybean	Early summer	1 lb.	Early fall

Provide a Good Soil Environment

The best plants are grown on soil that has met 3 major requirements. First, it must be acid (sour) and fertile. Second, it should have a lot of organic matter; and third, it must have good water drainage. If you don't have this kind of soil, don't get discouraged. You can change the soil so that you do have good soil for blueberries and we will tell you how to do it.

Making Soil Acid

The best soil pH (acidity) for growing blueberries is between pH 4.5 and 5.6. This is also good for rhododendrons and azaleas. If your soil is higher than 5.6, you should add powdered sulfur. You may have to experiment a little with amounts for your soil conditions. In general, 24 pounds of sulfur for each 1,000 square feet should lower acidity by 1 full pH point. If your pH is too low, your soil is too sour, and limestone should be added to sweeten it. Again, the exact amount will depend upon your location, but about 150 pounds per 1,000 square feet will raise the pH by 1 pH point.

There are several home soil test kits you can buy. These generally will indicate soil pH and fertility. However, because most of these rely upon color tests, you may have a difficult time interpreting them. You will probably be better off having your soil tested through your local county extension agent's office. There is usually only a modest charge for these services, and they will tell you how to take soil samples.

Increasing the Organic Matter

Blueberry soils should have a lot of organic matter. You can increase the level of organic material by adding compost, peat moss, leaves, straw, and other organic materials (except sewage sludge).

You must have good soil drainage with a water table no closer to the soil surface than 18 inches. A good way to test this yourself is simply to dig a hole about a foot deep and fill it with water. If the water disappears within about an hour and a half, the drainage is okay. If it doesn't you'd better find another spot. But remember, swampy areas can be planted as a last resort, if you either install a costly system of drainage ditches or plant the bushes on small mounds as they grow naturally in swamps.

Preparing the Soil

Preparing the soil for highbush blueberries means building up organic matter and adjusting the soil pH. The best way to start is to plant a green manure crop of buckwheat in the early summer prior to planting the blueberries the following spring. In late summer, measure the soil pH and adjust it to be between 4.5 and 5.0 by spreading either ground limestone (to raise the pH) or ground sulfur (to lower the pH) just before turning the buckwheat under. (Remember the formula: For loamy soil, add 24 pounds of sulfur per 1,000 square feet for each full pH point above 4.5. For sandy soil, decrease the rate to about 8 pounds per 1,000 square feet. For every full point you want to raise the pH, add about 150 pounds of limestone per 1,000 square feet.) In early September, till the area again, and plant a crop of winter rye. This will reduce soil loss from erosion during the winter months, as well as add additional organic matter. In early spring, turn under the winter rye and whatever other organic materials you can find — rotted manure, compost, and peat moss — and bring the soil to a fine texture by thorough harrowing or rototilling. Complete this and let the soil settle for at least 2 weeks before planting.

If you are only planting a few bushes, you can prepare individual planting holes. Dig the holes approximately 2 feet in diameter by 2 feet deep in the early spring. Use a mixture of equal parts of loam, sand, and organic matter, such as rotted sawdust, compost, or peat moss to fill the hole when planting. A word of caution! Be sure the sawdust or compost component of the mix is well rotted. Undecomposed organic matter, such as fresh sawdust, can severely stunt the plant.

Selecting Plants

Blueberry plants are available from nurseries as rooted cuttings or as older plants. Generally, we recommend buying dormant, vigorous 2-year-old plants, 12 to 18 inches high. Younger, smaller plants may be less expensive, but they require greater care, while the cost of older plants frequently is not justified. Obtain plants from a reputable nursery to assure trueness to name. To get the cultivars and quality that you want, place your order at least 6 months before planting.

Estimating Quantities

You can figure out how many bushes you need by remembering the following points:

- A plant 6 to 8 years old or older can produce up to 10 quarts of fruit per bush, if you take good care of it.
- Each mature bush may have a total spread of 4 to 5 feet.
- Bushes are usually spaced about 6 feet apart within rows and about 8 to 10 feet apart between rows.
- In hedgerows, space bushes 4 feet apart.

Blueberries are borne on 1-year-old shoots. Each overwintering flower bud can produce 5 to 15 berries, which typically ripen over a 6-week period.

Cultivars

Cultivar is just a shortened word for the term "cultivated variety." There are hundreds of different cultivars of highbush blueberries, and some will be best for you.

If you look in most seed catalogs, you will find that most mailorder operations will list only a few cultivars of blueberries. That's too bad, because cultivars have some definite geographic preferences. The list on the next 2 pages gives cultivars by region to help you choose the best variety. Even better than choosing from a list is enlisting the aid of your local county extension agent. These agents can tell you what cultivars other growers in your area have grown successfully.

You want to choose more than 1 cultivar to grow. Why? You will have a longer picking season and a better crop if you plant early, midseason, and late-ripening cultivars. Also, although blueberries are considered self-fruitful, you will get a greater yield and larger fruit that ripens earlier if you interplant several cultivars.

This listing is based on United States Department of Agriculture recommendations. Approximate order of ripening is indicated by the letters "e" for *early*, "m" for *midseason*, and "l" for *late*. There are **many** cultivars that are not included in this list, so **don't forget** to have that chat with your extension agent.

Geographic Area 1: North Florida, Coastal Plain of Georgia, South Carolina (south of Charleston), Louisiana, Mississippi, Alabama, East Texas, lower Southwest, and Southern California (Los Angeles and south)

Cultivars

Flordablue	Sharpblue (for trial only)

Geographic Area 2: Mountain and Upper Piedmont regions of Area 1

Cultivars

Morrow (e)	Patriot (m)
Croatan (e)	Bluecrop (m)
Harrison (e)	Berkeley (m)
Murphy (e)	Lateblue (l)
Bluetta (e)	

Geographic Area 3: Richmond, VA, south to Piedmont and Coastal Plain Carolinas, Tennessee, lower Ohio Valley, east and south Arkansas, lower Southwest, and mid-California

Cultivars

Morrow (e)	Bluecrop (m)
Croatan (e)	Patriot (except in coastal
Harrison (e)	plain areas) (m)
Murphy (e)	

Geographic Area 4: Mid-Atlantic states, Midwest, Ozark highlands, mountain regions of Area 3, northern California, Oregon, and Washington

Cultivars

Bluetta (e)	Darrow (l)
Collins (e)	Lateblue (l)
Patriot (m)	Elliott (l)
Bluecrop (m)	Herbert (l)
Blueray (m)	Elizabeth (l)
Berkeley (m)	

Geographic Area 5: New England and cooler areas of the Great Lakes States

Cultivars

Bluetta (e)	Blueray (m)
Collins (e)	Meader (m)
Patriot (m)	Berkeley (m)
Bluecrop (m)	Northland (m)

Planting

You can obtain blueberry plants from the nursery bare-rooted, canned (potted), or balled-and-burlapped. The latter 2 are best because they usually can be planted without disturbing the roots too much.

Bare-rooted plants often are shipped in plastic covers. Remove these as soon as the plants arrive. If you can't plant immediately, heel the plants in by placing the roots in a trench and mounding soil around them. If the ground is frozen, put them in a cool, protected place, such as a garage, and cover the entire plant with damp peat moss or sawdust.

Try to plant during the afternoon of a cloudy day.

Although blueberries can be planted in the fall, spring planting is safer and is recommended in most areas. Do this as soon as the ground can be worked in the spring. This means as soon as the ground has dried out enough. Prune off any damaged or excessively long roots, any weak or broken wood, and all flower buds, since fruiting the first year may stunt the bush.

Plant your bushes 1 to 2 inches deeper than they were in the nursery and 4 to 6 feet apart in rows spaced 8 to 10 feet apart. In large plantings, do not separate cultivars by more than 2 rows from others with similar ripening seasons. After you put the plants in the hole, fill it three-fourths full of either soil or a loam-peat-sand (1 to 1 to 1 proportions) mixture, and flood it with water. After the water has seeped out, fill the remainder of the hole and pack firmly with your feet. Water the plant thoroughly with a starter solution to encourage rapid growth.

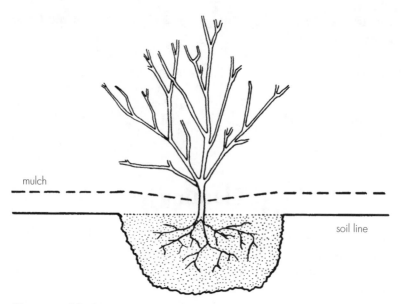

mulch

soil line

Plant your blueberry bush 1 to 2 inches deeper than it was planted in the nursery. Plant the bush in an oversized hole filled with a loam/peat/sand mixture.

Caring For Your Blueberries

Highbush blueberries are easy to grow. All you have to do is fertilize them 2 or 3 times a year, prune once a year, and make sure they have enough water. We will discuss their needs in this section. You always should pay attention to the general health — or as we call it, vigor — of your plants. A mature, vigorous bush should have dark green foliage and should produce 2 or 3 new shoots from the base of the plant each year. About half of the new growth on the bush should be longer than 5 or 6 inches and a few new shoots should be 12 to 18 inches long.

Irrigation

Blueberry plants require a constant moisture supply for best growth. The highbush blueberry plant has an exceedingly fine, fibrous root system that is mostly located within the dripline of the bush and within the top foot of soil. It is, therefore, relatively shallow and quite susceptible to drought stress under poor soil conditions.

When should you water? First, try the "feel test" to determine whether the soil needs moisture. Squeeze a soil sample in the palm of your hand. If the ball formed is weak and easily broken, soil moisture is adequate. If it is not easily broken, the soil is too wet; if no ball is formed, then it is too dry.

If irrigation is necessary, water during the early morning, but don't wet the bushes when berries are beginning to ripen. If you wet the berries at this time they may split. You can use ground flooding or soaker hose. This will conserve water and prevent wetting of the bush. Apply about an inch of water during each watering.

Pollination

As we mentioned earlier, blueberry plants are generally self-fruitful, but interplanting cultivars will improve yields because some cultivars, such as Earliblue and Coville, do not produce enough good pollen.

Bees are necessary for good cross-pollination. If the wild population is small, we recommend you provide 1 hive of bees for every 300 blueberry bushes. Bees should be introduced into the field

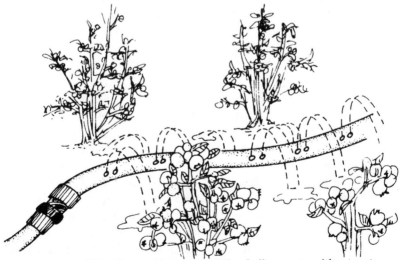

A soaker hose efficiently provides water to the shallow roots without wetting the berries, which could cause them to split.

Blueberries flower in early to late May, depending on the cultivar. The flowers are not especially tolerant of cold or frost.

before one-fourth of the earliest cultivar reaches full bloom. Place the hives near the center of each planting. If you are planning to do any insecticide spraying following bloom be sure to remove the bees.

Fertilization

All plants remove nutrients from the soil. If these are not replenished, the plant will soon lose vigor and crop production will be reduced. You can replace major nutrients by periodic application of recommended fertilizers.

We usually recommend fertilizers such as 5-10-10 or 10-10-10. Since these are more concentrated than "organic" fertilizers, they are applied in smaller quantities. We find that commercial fertilizers are more readily available, easier to handle, free from weed seeds, more consistent in nutrient content, and more readily available to the plant than organic materials, and that is why we prefer commercial fertilizers over "organic" ones.

Make the first fertilizer application about a month after planting. Apply about a half-cup of 5-10-10 or 10-10-10 per bush. Just spread the fertilizer around the plant in a broad band at least 6 inches but not more than 12 inches from its base. Repeat the application in early July. If the plants show low vigor, fertilize again in the fall when the leaves drop. Make the last 2 applications at the same rate as the first. If you have mulched around your bushes, double the rate of the first application and omit the second.

You should increase the rate of fertilizer each year until mature plants (after 6 to 8 years in the field) are receiving about 1 pound* per plant, two-thirds applied at the beginning of bloom and the other third applied 5 to 6 weeks later. Since most fertilizer nutrients move vertically in the soil, proper fertilizer placement is important.

If your mature plants are not vigorous, a late autumn application (when the leaves drop) of about 1 pound of fertilizer per bush will increase nutrient reserves in the plant and promote an early spurt of growth in the spring. Don't try this on your vigorous bushes, and do not apply the fertilizer too early in the autumn, since an early application could encourage late autumn shoot growth that will winterkill. When possible, rake in the fertilizer after application.

In sandy soil, where leaching is rapid, additional fertilizer may be required. This can, however, present a danger of root injury from the higher salt concentrations. You can offset poor growth in sandy soil by burying up to 3 bushels of a peat moss/soil mix (1 to 1 proportions) or compost per plant beneath the dripline — if you only have a few bushes to worry about. Plant roots will grow into these areas, invigorating the plant.

Be sure to fertilize every year regardless of whether a crop is produced.

You can use "organic" fertilizers if you want. Compounds such as blood meal, cottonseed meal, tankage, and well-rotted manure will provide some of the major nutrients. Most of these will also provide valuable organic material that will improve soil texture and aid plant growth. You should use combinations of these materials to provide for a more balanced fertilization. Don't use bone meal or wood ashes, because they tend to sweeten the soil.

---

* Complete fertilizers (10-10-10, 5-10-10, etc.) and superphosphate weigh about 7.5 oz. per cup; urea, ammonium sulfate, and ammonium nitrate weigh about 5.5 oz. per cup.

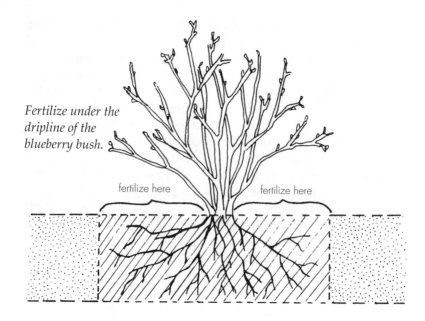

Fertilize under the dripline of the blueberry bush.

fertilize here   fertilize here

Don't apply organic fertilizers after the early summer, because they could stimulate late fall growth of the plants if applied too late. The amount to apply will be determined by the plant vigor.

Soil Management

Blueberry plants do not compete well with weeds for water and nutrients. Therefore, they should either be cultivated frequently or thoroughly mulched. In most areas of the country, mulching is perhaps the wisest and best soil management practice. We recommend it highly for the homeowner. Nearly any organic material — grass clippings, pine needles, straw, peat moss, buckwheat hulls, or wood chips — can be used.

Sawdust Mulch

We have used sawdust as a mulch very successfully for 35 years and strongly recommend it. Sawdust is a relatively inexpensive material. Like all organic mulches, it retains soil moisture, reduces soil temperature fluctuations, and adds valuable organic matter to the soil.

In addition, we have found that sawdust, in particular, substantially increases plant vigor and produces higher crop yields.

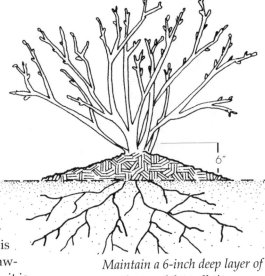

Maintain a 6-inch deep layer of sawdust mulch at all times.

The type of sawdust used does not matter. However, softwood sawdust is usually coarser in texture and decomposes more slowly than hardwood sawdust, and this is desirable. Although fresh sawdust can be used as a mulch, it is better to use aged material.

Apply the sawdust immediately after planting to soil that has been thoroughly moistened. Apply the mulch 4 inches deep and sloped toward the plant. Add additional mulch each year to build up and maintain a 6-inch depth at all times. The area beneath the plant or, preferably, the entire plantation can be mulched.

One bushel of moderately dry sawdust is equivalent to about two 5-gallon buckets, and weighs about 45 pounds. Plan to use about 5 bushels for each plant, depending on the size of the plant.

Breakdown of the sawdust will tie up some of the nitrogen in the soil. This may cause a nitrogen deficiency in the plant. To correct this, apply additional nitrogen fertilizer each time you add new mulch. We recommend the application of 2 pounds of ammonium nitrate or 6 pounds of 10-10-10 for each 100 pounds of sawdust mulch. You can correct nitrogen deficiencies with organic fertilizers that contain as little cellulose material as possible. Fish emulsion or blood meal are suitable. Exact quantities are dependent on the extent of the deficiency and the age of the plant. Remember, this is in addition to the regular fertilization.

Other Mulches

Some of the other organic mulches you can use may present particular problems which you should know about in advance. For example, grass clippings from lawns previously treated with herbicides should not be used. Peat moss, buckwheat hulls, and wood chips are relatively expensive, and the former may crust on the surface, restricting moisture penetration. Straw mulch may introduce weed seeds and present a considerable fire hazard. Inorganic materials such as black polyethylene, may also be suitable but have not been fully tested.

Hand Cultivation

If you choose to cultivate, start in the early spring and continue the practice as weeds grow throughout the growing season. Hand cultivation, with a hoe, should be very shallow (less than 1 inch) to avoid damaging the roots. Be careful not to knock fruit off the bush — ripening fruit drops especially easily. Since cultivated soil loses moisture more rapidly than mulched soil, be sure to water frequently enough to maintain enough soil moisture for good plant growth.

Pruning

There is a mystique to pruning fruit trees and bushes; it always seems to make gardeners nervous. But pruning is one of the important factors in developing and maintaining high production in your blueberry plantation. So let's eliminate some of the mystery by understanding the bearing habit of this plant.

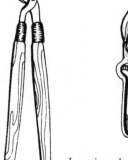

Most flower buds, each containing up to a dozen flowers, are produced at the tips of the current season's growth. They are formed during the summer and early fall for next year's bloom.

Lopping shears (left) is the best tool for removing large canes; hand shears (right) can be used for making fine cuts.

Since flower buds are only formed on new wood, stimulation of new growth through proper pruning and fertilization is necessary. Pruning should start immediately after planting and be continued each year in the early spring just as the flower buds begin to swell. The only tools needed will be a lopping shears, a hand shears, and maybe a handsaw.

Pruning at Planting

At planting time, you should remove all weak, diseased, and broken wood and all flower buds.

After One Year

Again prune any diseased or broken wood. Vigorous plants may be allowed to bear up to a pint of fruit (2 to 30 flower buds). Remove any additional buds.

Pruning a blueberry bush at planting.

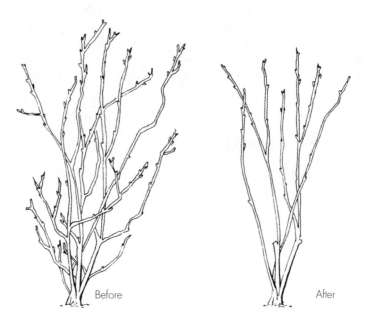

Pruning a blueberry bush after 2–5 years in the field.

After Two to Five Years

Continue similar pruning practices for the next 2 to 5 years. If the plants appear vigorous, do not remove more flower buds than is necessary during pruning. During this time, the emphasis should still be on producing healthy bushes and not on fruit production.

If well-grown bushes were started as healthy 2-year-old plants, they may be considered mature bushes after 6 to 8 growing seasons in the field.

Pruning Mature Bushes

After you have removed all dead and diseased wood, thin out the busy by removing one-fourth of the main branches. These can be cut at an angle slightly above the ground level or to a low, vigorous side shoot. This should be done each year, always removing the oldest canes. Branches older than 5 years are less productive. Failure to remove enough old wood, or inadequate fertilization, will

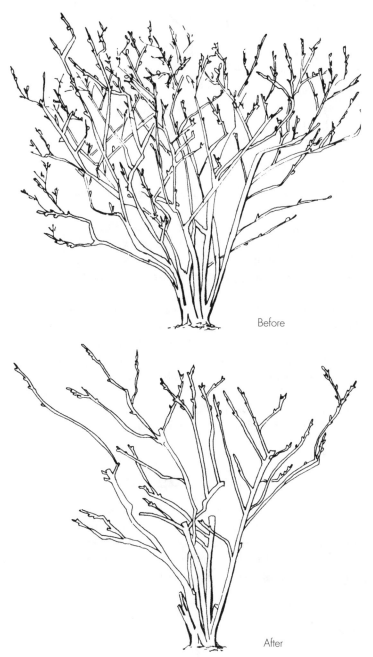

Before

After

Pruning a mature blueberry bush.

The heavy black marks indicate where cuts should be made to remove weak wood from a mature bush.

result in an insufficient number of new branches arising from the base of the bush.

After cutting out the main branches, thin the remainder of the bush, removing twiggy or bushy growth clusters, weak lateral shoots, and interfering branches. Unpruned bushes degenerate rapidly into a thick, twiggy mass of unfruitful wood.

Blueberry bushes that have been neglected for several years may be rejuvenated and returned to good production by severe pruning. Cut these back to the ground, leaving only short, 2-inch to 3-inch stubs. The whole bush may be done at once (1-year method) or half the bush may be done 1 year and the other half in the following year (2-year method). By using the 1-year method, the entire crop is lost for 1 season. The 2-year method does allow the plant to bear a portion of the crop each year of the rejuvenation process.

Propagation

You don't have to rely on expensive nursery stock for your new bushes. Blueberries can be propagated by many different methods. But, unless you are prepared to devote considerable time and effort to the process, the only methods we recommend are layering and mounding (stooling).

Layering

Layering is the simplest and the easiest method. Select a shoot of the current year's growth that is quite close to the ground, and

Layering

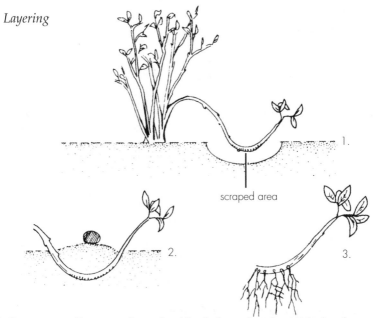

scraped area

1. Scrape a small area on the underside of a branch at least 5 inches from the growing tip. Bend the shoot to the ground and place the scraped portion in a 2-inch to 3-inch trench.
2. Fill the trench with soil and place a stone weight on top.
3. Rooting should be completed by late fall.

scrape a small (about 1-inch to 2-inch) area on the underside of the branch at least 5 inches from the growing tip. Bend the shoot to the ground and place the scraped portion in a 2-inch to 3-inch-deep trench. Cover with soil. To insure that the shoot will stay in this position, place a small stone on top. Some people prefer holding the shoot in place with bent wire. Make sure the growing tip is not covered. If this is done in the early spring, then rooting should be completed by late fall.

Air Layering

Air layering also is quite easy and it does not require shoots near the ground. In the late spring, scrape an area about 5 inches from the tip on a current year's shoot and wrap it in a ball of thoroughly moistened sphagum moss. Cover the moss with polyethylene and tie it above and below the sphagnum ball. The bottom tie should be

Air layering

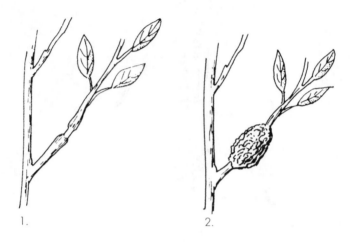

1. Remove a small portion of "bark" or make a small wound.
2. Cover the area with damp sphagnum moss.

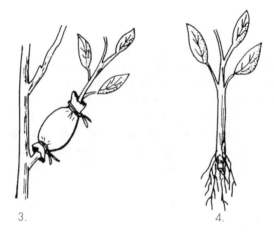

3. Cover the moss with plastic, tying tightly at top and fairly loosely at the
   bottom to allow for water drainage.
4. The area above the wound within the moss will root and can be sepa-
   rated from the rest of the plant.

Mounding

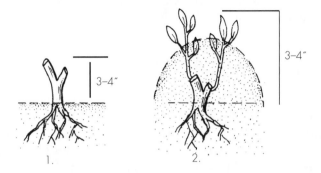

1. Cut the plant back to 3 to 4 inches.
2. When new shoots are 3 to 4 inches tall, mound the soil around them, allowing only 1 inch of the shoot to remain uncovered.

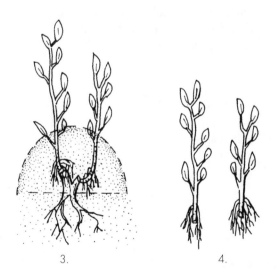

3. The shoots will be rooted by fall.
4. Cut off the rooted shoots and plant them. The stock can be used to propagate more shoots.

somewhat loose to allow for drainage of excess moisture. The sphagnum moss should remain damp until after rooting has taken place, which usually will be by early fall. Air-layered shoots should be planted in the fall.

Mounding

Mounding is usually done on the whole bush but an individual branch can be used. Branches are cut back to 3-inch or 4-inch stock in the early spring. When the new shoots which will develop from this stock are 3 or 4 inches tall, mound the soil around them allowing only about 1 inch of the shoot to remain uncovered. As in layering, shoots should be rooted by fall. When ready to plant, carefully wash the soil away from the plant, cut off rooted shoots, and plant them.

Hardwood Cuttings

The most common commercial propagating method is by hardwood cuttings. A small grower can use this method by constructing a miniature propagating box about 6 inches deep. Use hardware

Take a hardwood cutting during the dormant season from a vigorous shoot. The top cut is made ½ inch above a vegetative bud, and the bottom, slanted cut is made immediately below a bud.

flower bud

½ inch

vegetative bud

cloth for the bottom of the box and make sure that the box is at least 3 to 4 inches off the ground to provide good water drainage and aeration. Fill the box with a rooting medium of a 1 to 1 mixture of peat moss and sand. A support for a clear polyethylene cover for the box can be made from coat hangers or from thin pieces of wood.

Take wood for cuttings during the dormant season from vigorous shoots that grew the previous season. The top cut should be made about ½ inch above a bud and the bottom cut is preferably made on a slant immediately below a lower bud. Tip portion of shoots containing flower buds should not be used.

Store the cut shoots in damp peat moss or sand in a cool place until spring. Cut the shoots so that each cutting has 3 to 5 buds. Then insert the cuttings into the thoroughly wet propagating medium in the frame with only the top bud showing. After inserting cuttings, water the frame again to settle the mixture around the cuttings. *Do not use any fertilizer at this time.* Cover the frame with polyethylene and place it in a protected area away from direct sunlight. Water periodically. After the cuttings produce 2 to 4 inches of new growth, the shoots will temporarily stop growing (usually 6 to 10 weeks after starting the cutting). When shoot growth resumes, the cuttings should be fertilized with half-strength starter solution. Repeat fertilization at 10-day to 15-day intervals.

In the early fall, the rooted cuttings should be hardened off by removing the polyethylene cover for about 2 hours per day for the first week. Gradually, increase this time by an additional 3 to 4 hours every 3 to 4 days until the cover is removed completely. By this time, cuttings should be ready for spring planting. While they are still in the box, mulch them heavily during the first winter. Apply mulch after the first killing frost in the fall.

Protection From Birds

Birds present one of the worst problems of any pest. They are especially frustrating for the small grower in a suburban or other densely populated area. Nearly any kind of bird will destroy the ripening fruit and, at times, will even eat the flower buds on the plant. Nationally, blueberry crop lost to birds is estimated to be between 2 and 4 million dollars per year.

The blueberry's worst enemy is not insects or diseases, it is birds! Plastic netting, specifically for bird control, is shown here. Hardware cloth or chicken wire will also work well.

Many people are opposed to destruction of the birds. Since federal and state laws concerning shooting, trapping, and poisoning are quite complicated, and since these measures are not very effective, we will limit our discussion to alternative bird control methods.

Netting

The most effective type of bird control device is netting.

You can cover entire plantations or individual bushes for nearly 100 percent bird protection. A durable, synthetic netting, often made of nylon and treated to resist deterioration from ultraviolet radiation, will usually last for several seasons. Place the netting over the bushes as the first fruits begin to ripen, and remove it after harvest is completed. When protecting individual bushes, envelop the plant completely with the netting, tying the netting around the base of the plant and using scrap lumber supports to keep it off the bush. Whole plantations can be enclosed with netting, but it does require support posts and wires to keep the netting sufficiently high over the plants to allow easy access to the bushes. An alternative to the complete use of netting is to construct a "cage" for the plants from 1-inch-mesh poultry fencing. A combination of the 2 materials, with poultry fencing on the sides and flexible netting on the top, is quite frequently used.

Visual Repellents

Hawklike balloons, rubber snakes, and aluminum pie plates may be partially effective near the beginning of the ripening season. However, birds soon will become accustomed to these objects and will henceforth and forever after ignore them. In fact, it has been reported that some birds nest in the balloons and use them as strategic airbases from which to launch their midseason raids.

Auditory Repellents

One type of auditory repellent depends upon simple noisemakers, such as firecrackers, propane cannons, and radios. These are often placed on a timer, so that they are switched on at irregular intervals. Regular timing will frequently acclimate the birds to the timing of the sounds. They may then feed twice as fast between the noise sequences. A second type of auditory repellent depends upon the recordings of bird distress calls to frighten the pests. A third type utilizes the production of high frequency sounds to frighten the birds. This type appears to be the most effective of the auditory repellents.

Controlling Diseases and Insects

In many areas blueberries can be grown without the use of sprays. This is especially true if plants are maintained in vigorous condition, are planted in an optimum location, and are grown under good, sanitary conditions. This includes removing old leaves, berries, and prunings from the site and practicing good weed control. We have tried to maintain optimal conditions and have found that often no sprays, or only 1 to 2 sprays per year, were necessary. However, the pest problems may be more severe in some areas. This will require spray control measures.

Many people prefer not to use synthetic pesticides. We suggest that these people use a botanical insecticide, such as rotenone; a natural pest pathogen, such as *Bacillus thuringiensis;* a natural predator; or handpick the larger insect pests. Some of these control measures may not be very effective or may be too costly to use, in which case the grower will have to consider using a synthetic insecticide. In addition, if diseases are present, you will have to use a synthetic fungicide, if you want to produce any fruit at all.

All pesticides, including "organic" pesticides, have varying degrees of toxicity. Use all recommended precautions when applying these, and be sure they are stored in their original containers under lock and key at all times. Keep them out of the reach of children.

The degree of acute toxicity is indicated on the package by the label warning statement. Those compounds that are considered "highly toxic" have the words *DANGER* and *POISON* and a skull and crossbones on the label; we recommend you *never* use these. Moderately toxic compounds have the word *WARNING* on the label; slightly toxic compounds are labeled *CAUTION;* and relatively nontoxic compounds have no signal word on the label. Make sure you observe the specified time interval between last application and fruit harvest.

Important Diseases

Blueberry Stunt. Plants are stunted, with leaves turning first yellow, then brilliant red or mottled red in August or September. This symptom appears well before normal fall coloration. Berries are small and unpalatable. You can control this disease only by destroying infected plants and by controlling sucking insects which transmit this disease.

Stem Canker. New cankers appear in late summer as reddish swellings on new shoots. These swellings enlarge in the second year, lose their red color, and become fissured, blistered, and grayish. Eventually the cankers will girdle and kill the cane. Remove infected branches and maintain plants in good vigor.

Mummyberry. Ripening fruit turns a creamy pinkish color instead of blue. Berries shrivel, become hard and dry, and drop to the ground. They provide an overwintering body for the fungus. Spring rains provide for the release of the fungus, which then attacks the new growth and swelling buds. This is the "twig blight" stage of the disease, which is recognized by blackened and wilted new growth. Additional spores produced in this stage infect the flowers and fruit, thus completing the cycle. Controlling this disease may require several applications of a fungicide such as Funginex. Apply this just as the flower buds begin to swell in the spring. Additional applications of fungicide may be required. Follow label directions. Also, applying at least 2 inches of additional mulch will help control this disease.

Botrytis Blight. New growth in the spring appears watersoaked and discolored. Later, some may become covered with grayish-white mold. Often infection begins in the flower, moves into the fruit cluster and then into the shoot, resulting in a few inches of shoot dieback. Leaves may become infected when they contact infected flowers or shoots. Very little infection occurs late in the season.

Apply Ferbam, Captan, or Benlate just as the buds show green, but before the blossoms open. Removal of fallen blueberry leaves may also help control this disease.

Witches Broom. The disease appears on the shoots only, producing a "broomlike" development of many deformed shoots arising close together on a swollen stem. This disease is found on the edges of woodlands where the balsam fir is present. This fit is an alternate host for the disease. Eliminate the nearby balsam fir trees and remove infected plants.

Red Ringspot Virus. The symptoms become very obvious in the autumn, when characteristic red, often irregular, rings appear on the leaves. Rings may also appear on the stems. Removing affected plants is the only control.

Insects

Tip Borer. Newly hatched worms bore into the soft, new stems of the plant. The tunnels may reach 6 to 10 inches in length by autumn and destroy the stem. New shoots will wilt, arch over, and discolor, with leaves turning yellow with red veins. Stems will turn purple. Prune off affected shoot tips and begin applying malathion, methoxychlor, or rotenone sprays when blossoms begin to drop.

Red-Banded Leaf Roller. The greenish larvae feed on foliage during the early summer, often folding or rolling leaves together. Later larvae feed on the fruit surface near the stem. Pupae overwinter and moths emerge in the spring to lay eggs on the plant bark in flattened clusters. Most leaf rollers can be controlled with malathion, methoxychlor, or rotenone sprays beginning when about three-fourths of the blossoms have fallen. These may have to be repeated over a 4-week to 5-week period.

Sharp-Nosed Leafhopper. The adult is dark chocolate in color with a pointed extension of the head. Eggs begin hatching in mid-spring and adults develop in early summer. This insect is very important, not so much for its actual feeding damage, but because it is the only known agent capable of transmitting blueberry stunt disease. Control these as you would the leaf rollers.

Scale. The winged adult is about $\frac{1}{25}$ inch in length and bronze in color. The female secretes a grayish-brown waxy covering which envelops and protects her. The young (crawlers) move to other sites and begin to feed by sucking the plant juices. Further development takes place, and the scale overwinters under its waxy protection. Development begins anew when spring temperatures reach 50°F. Feeding injury appears as red specks on the plant part, usually a shoot. The plant will usually decline in vigor and productivity in cases of severe infestation. Control with delayed dormant sprays of 60 to 70 sec. spray oil and remove heavily infested branches.

A delayed dormant spray is one that is applied when the buds have begun to swell, but before any amount of leaf or flower tissue has emerged. A spray oil is a refined petroleum product (oil) especially marketed for use on plants. Most of these are sold as spray oils and are listed as "60 or 70 sec." The numbers refer to a viscosity rating. The lower the number, the less viscous (thinner) the oil.

Blossom Weevil. The long-snouted adult beetle emerges in the spring and begins feeding on the plant, boring into the side of swelling buds and flowers. Injured buds usually do not open, or they open deformed. Egg-laying begins during bloom, when the female weevil punctures the flower to place the eggs. Hatching in a few days, the grub eats the flower, often destroying over half of the crop. Begin control treatment with malathion when flower buds show white.

Cherry Fruitworm. The adult dark gray moth emerges in late spring, and lays its eggs on the undersides of leaves and on the fruit. These hatch in about a week, and the larvae enter the fruit through the blossom end and feed on the pulp for a few weeks. Larvae will hibernate in pithy weeds or small prunings near the base of the bush. Control is the same as suggested for leaf roller.

Cranberry Fruitworm. The night-flying adult moths become active when the largest berries are about one-fourth grown and lay eggs in the blossom end of the fruit. In about a week, the young green caterpillars hatch and enter a berry. Up to 6 fruit may be webbed together during feeding. Following feeding, the mature caterpillar crawls to the ground and overwinters in a soil-encrusted cocoon under weeds or trash. Control as suggested for leaf roller.

Plum Curculio. The adult beetle has a long snout and is brown to steely gray with whitish patches. It has 4 bumps on its wing. Beetles usually become active when early cultivars begin to bloom. The adults feed on buds and flowers, making a small hole about ⅛ inch deep. When berries are about ¼ inch in diameter, the female laying eggs in the fruit. Punctures in the fruit in which eggs are laid are typically half-moon or crescent shaped. The eggs hatch in late summer in about 6 days, and the worm feeds on the fruit. Infested berries usually fall to the ground, worms remain in the berries for about 3 weeks, and then move into soil. After about a month, new moths emerge to feed on the foliage before moving into trash or soil to winter over. Control with malathion, as suggested for leaf roller.

Blueberry Maggot. The adults become active in midsummer. They resemble houseflies except for their characteristic black wing bands. The female punctures the fruit skin to lay her eggs. After a short period, the eggs hatch into small maggots which feed on the flesh of the fruit. The berries will often decay or ripen prematurely and become inedible. In mid-June, apply carbaryl or malathion, and continue spraying at recommended intervals.

Yellow-Necked Caterpillar, Acronicta Caterpillar. Caterpillars need little description, but the damage they do by chewing the leaves cannot go unattended. Handpick the colonies.

Fall Webworm. The pale yellow, black-spotted hairy caterpillar forms large colonies in a tightly spun web. Caterpillars feed on foliage inside the web until it is consumed, then make another web. Handpick the colonies.

Stem Borer. Grubs emerging during warm weather bore into the stems about 3 to 6 inches from the tip. If left undisturbed, they will emerge as large, conspicuous, long-horned beetles after 3 years. The infested canes will have small piles of sawdust near their bases and will appear weakened. Remove the wilted canes below the injured area. Do this as soon as injury appears.

Control recommendations are subject to change. Always follow specific directions listed on the pesticide package. For further information, contact your local agricultural extension agent. When trade names are used for identification of control measures, no product endorsement is implied, nor is discrimination intended against similar materials. The user of this information assumes all risks for personal injury or property damage.

Harvesting

To get the highest quality berries, harvest 4 to 6 days after the berry turns completely blue. If picked earlier, the berries will not be as large and the flavor will not be fully developed. Berries picked when not completely ripe will ripen off the bush, but they will be of poorer quality. Since overripe berries shrivel and may drop, the entire planting should be harvested about once a week, or more frequently during high temperatures.

Since harvesting goes more quickly if both hands are free for picking, tie a container around your neck or attach it to your belt.

Resource

Indiana Berry & Plant Co.
5218 W 500 S
Huntingburg, IN 47542-9724
Plants and Products for the Small Fruit Grower
(800) 295-2226
www.inberry.com